Contents

FUN FOOD
for kids'
lunches - snacks - meals

NEW
HOLLAND

INTRODUCTION

This is a cookbook with a difference: the recipes were chosen by children for children, children helped to test them, and it was the majority view that decided what should be included.

The result is a well-balanced selection of recipes for all ages and all occasions. Brains with parsley sauce and tripe and onions got the thumbs down, but the panel approved plenty of salads, wholefood bakes, fruity desserts and vegetarian dishes alongside old favourites like kebabs, pizza, pasta, chicken drumsticks and sweet treats such as rocky road ice cream and lamingtons.

Breakfasts and lunches came in for careful scrutiny, with the accent on speedily prepared dishes for school days and some special treats for weekends. Dinners are more substantial, but also take into account the pit-stop factor—some dishes can be made in minutes while others can safely be put on hold for latecomers.

Healthy school lunches are an important part of helping your kids make the most of their school day—they need good food to help them grow, learn and play.

Their day should, however, be a mix of learning and fun, so what they find in their lunchboxes should not only be healthy but also something they look forward to. It can also be a place to help slowly develop their idea of flavour as an adventure.

Keeping it fresh, simple and healthy is the key to a fun lunchtime for all.

Fast and Simple

This chapter focuses on getting the lunches made as fast as possible on those days where there is no extra time to prepare more complicated foods. The idea is to keep the kids happy and healthy but not late for school! With minimum preparation, they will be heading off with a lunch box full of goodness to see them through the day.

Tuna Wraps

6oz (185g) canned tuna,
  drained

2 tablespoons mayonnaise

¼ avocado, diced

1 spring onion, finely sliced

1 iceberg lettuce leaf,
  finely shredded

1 piece mountain bread or
  flat bread

1. Combine tuna, mayonnaise, avocado and spring onion. Stir together.
2. Place lettuce on the mountain bread and top with the tuna mixture. Roll tightly and cut in half.

Serves 1

Pita Pockets

1 wholemeal pita pocket

2 tablespoons hummus

¼ medium carrot, grated

1 tablespoon Cheddar cheese, grated

1 small cooked beetroot, grated

²/₃oz (20g) lettuce leaves, shredded

1 tablespoon raisins or sultanas

1 teaspoon lemon juice

1. Cut pita pocket in half, spread each half with the hummus.
2. Mix the remaining ingredients in a bowl. Divide the mixture between each pocket.

Serves 1

French Toast

1 egg
¼ cup milk
1 teaspoon sugar
½ teaspoon vanilla extract
2 slices wholemeal bread
¼ teaspoon ground cinnamon

1. Place egg, milk, sugar and vanilla into a flat dish, whisk with a fork.
2. Place bread into egg mixture and leave 1–2 minutes.
3. Heat a non-stick frying pan, place the bread into the pan and allow to brown before turning to brown other side. Sprinkle with cinnamon and serve with fresh fruit.

Serves 1–2

Turkey and Cranberry Sandwich

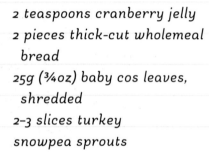

2 teaspoons cranberry jelly

2 pieces thick-cut wholemeal
  bread

25g (¾oz) baby cos leaves,
  shredded

2–3 slices turkey

snowpea sprouts

1. Spread the cranberry jelly over the bread. Place the lettuce, turkey slices and sprouts on 1 slice of bread. Top with the remaining piece of bread and cut in half.

Makes 1

Lavash Wrap

1 piece wholemeal lavash
  bread
2 teaspoons wholegrain
  mustard
¾oz (25g) rocket (arugula)
1 slice ham
1 tablespoon ricotta cheese

1. Spread lavash with mustard, top with rocket and ham. Crumble over the ricotta.
2. Roll up the lavash, then cut in half.

Makes 1

Egg and Cheese Sandwiches

2 eggs, hard-boiled

1 thick-sliced Cheddar cheese, diced

1 sprig parsley, roughly chopped

1 tablespoon mayonnaise

2 slices thick-sliced wholegrain bread

1. In a small bowl, mash the egg, add the cheese, parsley and mayonnaise. Mix together.

2. Spread the egg and cheese mixture onto one slice of bread, top with the other slice and cut into quarters.

Serves 1

White Bean Dip

14oz (400g) canned cannellini
  beans
1 clove garlic, crushed
¼ cup extra virgin olive oil
juice of ½ lemon

1. Rinse and drain the beans. Place the beans, garlic, olive oil, and lemon juice in a food processor and process until combined. Add 1 tablespoon of water and process again until smooth.
2. Serve with a selection of mini toasts, rice crackers, carrot sticks and celery sticks.

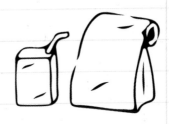

Pasta Salad

¾ cup cooked pasta such as
  spirals or penne
1 tablespoon sweetcorn
  kernels
8 cherry tomatoes, halved
1 tablespoon pepitas (pumpkin
  seeds)
1 sprig parsley, roughly
  chopped
1oz (30g) Cheddar cheese,
  cubed
¹/₃oz (10g) baby spinach
½ tablespoon olive oil
1 teaspoon lemon juice

1. Combine all ingredients in a bowl and mix well.
   Store in an airtight container.

Serves 1

Cherry Tomato and Baby Bocconcini Salad

8 cherry tomatoes, halved

4 baby bocconcini, halved

¼ Lebanese cucumber, thickly
  sliced

1 scallion (spring onion),
  sliced

1 sprig parsley, chopped

1 teaspoon olive oil

1. Combine all ingredients in a bowl and mix thoroughly.

Serves 1

Waldorf Salad

1 green apple, cut into chunks

1 red apple, cut into chunks

1 stalk celery, sliced

5 baby cos leaves, finely shredded

¼ cup mayonnaise

1 teaspoon lemon juice

¼ cup pecan or walnut halves

1. Combine the apples, celery and lettuce in a bowl with the mayonnaise, lemon juice and pecans or walnuts. Mix well.

Serves 4

Apricot and Coconut Balls

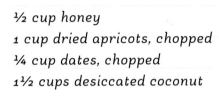

½ cup honey
1 cup dried apricots, chopped
¼ cup dates, chopped
1½ cups desiccated coconut

1. Place honey, apricots, dates and 1 cup of coconut in a food processor, process together.
2. Roll heaped tablespoonfuls of mixture into balls and roll in the remaining coconut. Store in the refrigerator.

Makes 12

Fruit Bubble Bumps

7oz (200g) butter

4 tablespoons honey

4½ cups rice bubbles or
 rice krispies

½ cup dates, chopped

¼ cup dried apple, chopped

1. Line a 12-cup muffin tray with coloured cupcake cases.
2. Bring butter and honey to the boil in a small saucepan, simmer for 5 minutes.
3. Combine the rice bubbles and chopped fruit in a large bowl. Pour over the butter mixture and stir to combine.
4. Divide mixture between the cupcake cases. Refrigerate until firm. Store in an airtight container to keep fresh.

Makes 12

Friendly Classics

Here we offer you tried and tested classics, without any extra fat and low on processed foods. Lunchtime standards with a healthy twist—if it's white bread, then it's packed full of fibre. Kid-friendly foods that they love and recognise, and that you know are doing the best for their growing bodies and minds. These lunches are yummy enough for them to ask for and healthy enough for you to give them, over and over again.

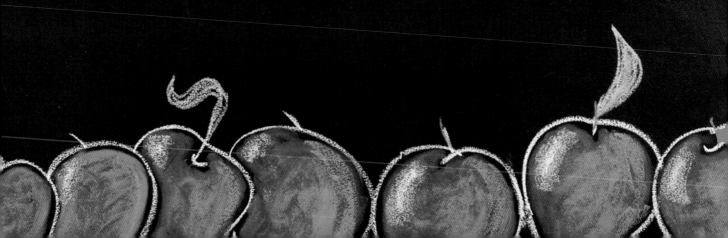

Hummus with Pita Chips

10½oz (300g) chickpeas,
  cooked
1 clove garlic, crushed
¼ cup extra virgin olive oil
1 tablespoon tahini
½ teaspoon ground cumin
juice of ½ lemon

PITA CHIPS
2 small pita pockets
olive oil spray

1. Preheat oven to 350°F (180°C).
2. Place the chickpeas, garlic, olive oil, tahini, cummin and lemon juice in a food processor and process until combined. Add 1 tablespoon of water and process again until quite smooth.
3. Cut the pita pockets in half horizontally, then cut each half into 6 triangles. Place on a baking tray and spray with oil. Bake for 10 minutes.

Serves 4

Chicken and Mayonnaise Baguette

1 small cooked chicken breast,
  diced
1 tablespoon walnuts, chopped
1 tablespoon mayonnaise
1 tablespoon sour cream
¼ small bunch chives,
  chopped
1 baguette, halved
1¾oz (50g) baby cos lettuce

1. Combine chicken, walnuts, mayonnaise, sour cream and chives in a bowl and mix well.
2. Cut the two baguette pieces in half horizontally. Divide the lettuce between the two baguette pieces and top each with the chicken mixture.

Makes 2

Ham and Swiss Sandwich

4 *slices high-fibre white bread*
1 *tablespoon tomato chutney*
4 *slices leg ham*
2 *slices Swiss cheese*

1. Lay out two slices of bread, spread on the chutney.
2. Divide the ham and Swiss cheese between the 2 slices. Top with remaining slices of bread, then cut into triangles.

Makes 2

Cheesy Vegetable Muffins

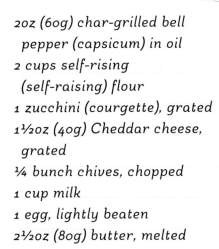

2oz (60g) char-grilled bell
   pepper (capsicum) in oil
2 cups self-rising
   (self-raising) flour
1 zucchini (courgette), grated
1½oz (40g) Cheddar cheese,
   grated
¼ bunch chives, chopped
1 cup milk
1 egg, lightly beaten
2½oz (80g) butter, melted

1. Preheat oven to 400°F (200°C). Lightly butter a 12-cup muffin tray.
2. Place the pepper on absorbent paper to drain off any excess oil. Slice the capsicum.
3. Sift the flour into a large bowl. Add the pepper, courgette, Cheddar and chives. Stir well to combine, then make a well in the centre. Use a fork to whisk the milk, egg and butter together in a large jug. Add to the flour mixture and use a large wooden spoon to mix until just combined—don't over-mix.
4. Divide the mixture evenly between the muffin cups. Bake for 20–25 minutes or until a skewer inserted into the centre of the muffins comes out clean. Set aside for 5 minutes before turning onto a wire rack.

Makes 12

Egg and Tuna Salad

4 cocktail potatoes, cut in half

2 eggs, soft-boiled and
   quartered

6oz (185g) canned tuna,
   drained

10 cherry tomatoes, halved

1¾oz (50g) green beans

2 scallions (spring onions),
   chopped

1 sprig parsley, roughly
   chopped

1 tablespoon mayonnaise

1. Cook potatoes until tender. Drain and leave to
   cool.
2. Combine potatoes and egg in a bowl, add
   remaining ingredients and gently stir.

Serves 2

Tropical Pizza

2 small pizza bases
¼ cup tomato pasta sauce
2 slices leg ham
3½oz (100g) pineapple, diced
2oz (60g) Cheddar cheese,
   grated
2 sprigs oregano, leaves
   removed and chopped

1. Preheat oven to 350°F (180°C).
2. Spread pizza bases with the tomato sauce. Top with the ham and pineapple, then the cheese and oregano. Bake for 15-20 minutes until golden brown.

Serves 4

Salami Scrolls

2 cups self-rising (self-raising) flour

1oz (30g) butter, chilled

¾ cup milk

¼ cup tomato paste (concentrate)

1 sprig basil, chopped

1 sprig parsley, chopped

3½oz (100g) salami, diced

1 medium red bell pepper (capsicum), diced

5oz (150g) Cheddar cheese, grated

1. Preheat oven to 350°F (180°C) and line an oven tray with baking paper.
2. Place flour and butter in a bowl, use fingers to combine until it resembles breadcrumbs. Add the milk and mix together to make a soft, sticky dough. Knead lightly on a floured surface.
3. Roll dough into a 30 x 40cm (12 x 15¾in) rectangle. Spread the tomato paste over the dough, sprinkle the chopped herbs on top. Top with the salami, pepper and cheese.
4. Roll up from the long side of the dough. Using a serrated knife, cut the roll into 12 slices. Place the slices on the oven tray and bake for 25 minutes until brown.

Makes 12

Bacon and Egg Pies

3 sheets ready-rolled puff
  pastry
17½oz (500g) bacon, thinly
  sliced
1½ cups sour cream
¼ cup parsley, chopped
12 eggs

1. Preheat oven to 400°F (200°C) and lightly butter a 12-cup Texas muffin tray.
2. Cut pastry sheets into quarters. Place a square of pastry into each muffin cup.
3. Cook bacon in a frying pan for 3-4 minutes or until light golden. Drain on absorbent paper and cool for 5 minutes. Divide three-quarters of bacon evenly between the pastry shells.
4. Whisk sour cream and parsley until well combined, then pour over bacon. Crack an egg on top of each pie, then top with remaining bacon.
5. Bake for 25-30 minutes or until pastry is golden and filling is cooked. Stand for 5 minutes before removing from pan. Serve hot or cold.

Makes 12

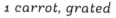

Chicken and Vegetable Rolls

1 carrot, grated
1 courgette (zucchini), grated
1 small onion, finely diced
9oz (250g) minced chicken
½ cup breadcrumbs
4 sprigs chives, chopped
1 egg, beaten
2 sheets ready-rolled puff
  pastry
1 tablespoon milk
1 tablespoon sesame seeds

1. Preheat oven to 400°F (200°C) and line an oven tray with baking paper.
2. In a large bowl, combine carrot, zucchini, onion, chicken mince, breadcrumbs, chives and egg.
3. Place pastry sheets on a floured surface and halve. Spoon quarter of the chicken mixture lengthwise along centre of each piece. Fold 1 edge of pastry over and tuck in beside filling, then fold over other side to make a roll, pressing down lightly to seal. Repeat with the remaining pastry and filling. Cut rolls into 3cm (1¼in) pieces, place on baking sheet, brush with milk and sprinkle with sesame seeds.
4. Bake for 25–30 minutes until the rolls are lightly browned and cooked through.

Makes 20

Banana Muffins

1¾ cups wholemeal self-rising
  (self-raising) flour
¾ cup firmly packed brown
  sugar
¼ cup walnut pieces
2 bananas, mashed
1 egg, lightly beaten
1 cup buttermilk
²/₃oz (20g) butter, melted

1. Preheat oven to 350°F (180°C) and lightly butter a 12-cup muffin tray.
2. Sift flour and sugar into a bowl, stir through the walnut pieces. Mix banana, egg, buttermilk and butter in a separate bowl. Add to the dry ingredients and stir to just combine.
3. Divide mixture between muffin cups and bake for 20-25 minutes. Test with a skewer to make sure muffins are cooked. Leave to cool for 5 minutes, then turn onto a cooling rack.

Makes 12

Muesli Bars

½ cup desiccated coconut
½ cup sesame seeds
1 cup rolled oats
½ cup sunflower seeds
½ cup raisins or sultanas
½ cup currants
1 cup dried apricots,
 finely chopped
1 cup dates, finely chopped
¾ cup orange juice
2 tablespoons honey

1. Preheat oven to 350°F (180°C) and line a 23cm (9in) square cake tin with baking paper.
2. Combine coconut, sesame seeds, rolled oats and sunflower seeds in a bowl, mix well, then spread out evenly on a baking tray. Bake for 10 minutes or until toasted, then transfer to a bowl.
3. Combine raisins, currants, apricots, dates, orange juice and honey in a saucepan. Bring to the boil and simmer for 2 minutes. Cool the mixture and combine with the toasted mixture.
4. Press into tin. Refrigerate overnight before cutting into bars.

Makes 12

Special Food

Not everyone can eat the same foods, so we have provided a chapter of dairy- and wheat-free recipes for those who may have these common food intolerances. Of course, these recipes are still very healthy and add more options to your lunch repertoire, so even if your child has no dietary restrictions, these recipes are a great way to add some variety to their lunchbox.

Beetroot Dip

1 medium beetroot, root and
  stem trimmed
1 cup natural yoghurt
2 cloves garlic, crushed
1 sprig fresh thyme, leaves
  removed and stalk discarded
pinch of salt

1. Place the unpeeled beetroot in a medium
   saucepan and cover with plenty of cold water.
   Bring to the boil, reduce heat to medium and
   cook for 20 minutes or until tender. Drain and
   set aside until cool enough to handle.

2. Wear gloves to avoid staining your hands, and
   peel the beetroot. Set aside until cooled to room
   temperature. Cut the beetroot into large pieces,
   place in a food processor and process until
   smooth. Add the yoghurt, garlic and thyme, and
   process until well combined. Season with salt.
   Serve with carrot and celery sticks. Keep any
   leftover dip in the refrigerator.

Serves 4

Brown Rice Salad

¾ cup brown rice
1 tablespoon pine nuts, toasted
¹/₃ cup sunflower seeds
1 teaspoon ground cumin
2 tablespoons currants
1 scallion (spring onion), sliced
2 sprigs cilantro (coriander), chopped

DRESSING
zest of ½ orange
1 tablespoon fresh orange juice
1 tablespoon olive oil

1. Bring a pot of water to the boil, add the brown rice and cook for 25-30 minutes until tender. Drain, rinse under cold running water, drain again and place in a large bowl.
2. Add pine nuts, sunflower seeds, cumin, currants, scallion and cilantro.
3. To make dressing, place all ingredients in a small bowl, whisk to combine and pour over the salad.

Serves 4

Shredded Chicken and Cabbage Salad

1 cooked chicken breast,
  shredded

1/8 red cabbage, finely
  shredded

¼ baby wombok, finely
  shredded

1 carrot, grated

2 sprigs parsley, chopped

1 orange

½ teaspoon Dijon mustard

2 tablespoons oil

1. Combine chicken, red cabbage, wombok, carrot and parsley in a bowl mix well.
2. With a sharp knife, peel the orange to remove all skin and pith, and trim away the outer skin on the segments. Working over a bowl to save the juices, remove the segments by cutting along either side of each segment, between the skin and the flesh. Add the segments to the chicken and cabbage.
3. Combine the orange juice, mustard and oil and pour over the salad.

Serves 4

Pumpkin and Fig Salad

9oz (250g) butternut pumpkin,
 cut into ¾in (2cm) pieces
1 teaspoon ground cumin
2 tablespoons olive oil
salt
7oz (200g) canned garbanzo
 beans (chickpeas), drained
 and rinsed
4 dried figs, chopped
½ small red onion, thinly
 sliced
1¾oz (50g) baby spinach
2 sprigs parsley, chopped
1 tablespoon lemon juice

1. Preheat oven to 400°F (200°C). Combine
   pumpkin, cumin and 1 tablespoon of the oil in a
   bowl. Season with salt and place in a roasting
   dish. Roast for 10 minutes or until tender, then
   allow to cool.
2. Combine pumpkin, chickpeas, figs, onion,
   spinach and parsley in a large bowl. Toss until
   well combined. Pour over the lemon juice and
   remaining oil before packing into lunchbox.

Serve 4

Quinoa Salad

¼ cup quinoa
1oz (30g) green beans,
  cut into ¾in (2cm) pieces
1 tomato, diced
¼ cup mint, finely chopped
1 tablespoon olive oil
1 teaspoon lemon juice

1. Rinse quinoa in cold water. Drain and place in a saucepan with ½ cup water, bring to the boil and simmer for 10 minutes until tender. Drain and cool.
2. Bring a small pot of water to the boil and blanch the beans, drain and refresh.
3. Mix the tomato, mint and beans through the quinoa. Stir through the oil and lemon juice.

Serves 4

Buckwheat Noodle Salad

1¾oz (50g) buckwheat noodles

1oz (30g) snowpeas, cut into
  thin strips

1 small carrot, cut into thin
  sticks

¼ red bell pepper (capsicum),
  cut into
  thin slices

¼ green bell pepper
  (capsicum), cut into thin
  slices

1 teaspoon sesame oil

½ teaspoon sesame seeds

2 sprigs cilantro (coriander),
  chopped

1. Bring a pot of water to the boil, add the buckwheat noodles and cook for 5 minutes or until just firm in the centre (al dente). Rinse under cold water and drain, then transfer to a bowl

2. Add the remaining ingredients and mix well. Serve in a noodle box.

Serves 2

Corn Bread

½ teaspoon olive oil

1 red bell pepper (capsicum),
 finely chopped

1 teaspoon ground cumin

1¼ cups gluten-free self-
 rising (self-raising) flour

¾ cup cornmeal (polenta)

1 teaspoon baking powder

½ teaspoon salt

4oz (125g) corn kernels

¼ cup cilantro (coriander),
 finely chopped

1 cup soymilk

1½oz (40g) dairy-free spread
 (Nuttelex), melted and cooled

1 egg, lightly whisked

1. Preheat oven to 420°F (220°C) and lightly spray an 8 x 21cm (3¼ x 8¼in) loaf tin with olive oil spray.

2. Heat oil in a non-stick frying pan over medium-high heat. Add capsicum and cook, stirring, for 5 minutes or until capsicum is tender. Add cumin and cook, stirring, for 1 minute or until aromatic. Set aside for 5 minutes to cool slightly.

3. Combine the flour, cornmeal, baking powder and salt in a large bowl. Add the corn, cilantro and bell pepper mixture, and stir until well combined. Add the soymilk, melted dairy-free spread and egg, and use a wooden spoon to mix until well combined.

4. Pour into the loaf tin and smooth surface with the back of a spoon. Bake for 30-35 minutes or until a skewer inserted into the centre of the loaf comes out clean. Stand for 5 minutes before turning onto a wire rack.

Makes 1 loaf

Bean and Bacon Salad

1oz (30g) green beans,
  cut in to ¾in (2cm) pieces

3 rashers bacon, sliced

7oz (200g) canned cannellini
  beans

7oz (200g) canned borlotti
  beans

½ red onion, finely chopped

8 cherry tomatoes, quartered

¼ cup parsley, chopped

¼ cup mint, chopped

DRESSING

1 teaspoon wholegrain
  mustard

2 tablespoons orange juice

2 tablespoons olive oil

1. Bring a pot of water to the boil, blanch beans, refresh in cold water and place in a bowl.
2. Fry bacon until golden brown, then drain on absorbent paper. Add to the beans.
3. Rinse and drain the cannellini and borlotti beans, add to the bacon and green beans. Add the onion, tomato, parsley and mint. Mix to combine.
4. To make dressing, whisk ingredients together in a bowl. Serve dressing in a separate container in the lunchbox.

Serves 4

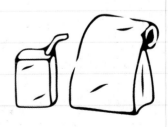

Rice Paper Rolls

1¾oz (50g) vermicelli rice
   noddles
1 carrot, cut into thin strips
1 cucumber, deseeded and
   cut into thin strips
½ cup cilantro (coriander)
1 tablespoon sweet chilli
   sauce
3½oz (100g) organic firm tofu,
   cut into strips
16 small rice paper sheets

1. Soak noodles in boiling water for 5 minutes until soft, then drain and place in a bowl.
2. Add carrot, cucumber, cilantro and sweet chilli sauce and mix.
3. Pour hot water in a shallow bowl, place rice paper in the water for about 30 seconds until soft. Gently lift out and place on a clean surface.
4. In the centre of 1 wrapper, place some noodle mix and top with some of the tofu strips. Roll the rice paper, sealing with a little water. Place on a tray and cover with a clean, damp tea towel to keep moist. Repeat with the remaining rice paper sheets.

Makes 16

Fruit Salad

4oz (125g) strawberries, halved

¼ pineapple, cut into chunks

1 banana, cut into chunks

½ mango, cut into chunks

4oz (125g) blueberries

2 passionfruit

juice of 1 orange

1 sprig mint, chopped

1. Place the strawberries, pineapple, banana, mango and blueberries in a bowl.
2. Cut the passionfruit in half, scoop out the pulp and add to the fruit. Pour over the orange juice and mix in the mint leaves.

Serves 2

Flourless Orange Cake

2 oranges

3 eggs

1 cup superfine (caster) sugar

3 cups almond flour (meal)

1 teaspoon gluten-free
baking powder

1. Preheat oven to 338°F (170°C), lightly butter and line a round 22cm (8½in) springform pan.

2. Place the unpeeled oranges in a saucepan and cover with cold water. Bring to the boil over medium heat. Cook for 15 minutes or until tender. Drain, then return to pan and cover with cold water. Bring to the boil and cook for 15 minutes. Drain and chop oranges, discard any seeds. Place oranges in a food processor and process until smooth.

3. Use an electric beater to whisk the eggs and sugar in a bowl until thick and pale. Add the oranges, almond meal and baking powder and gently fold until just combined. Pour into prepared pan.

4. Bake for 1 hour. Test with a skewer to make sure cake is cooked. Set aside for 15 minutes to cool, then cut into wedges to serve.

Summer Snacks

Summer is a time of abundant fresh foods, full of natural taste and natural sugars, so let's take advantage of all those fruits and vegetables available for the choosing. In this chapter we focus on fresh summer food while ensuring that the lunches will also travel well on a hot day—food that can handle a bit of heat and still remain healthy and tasty.

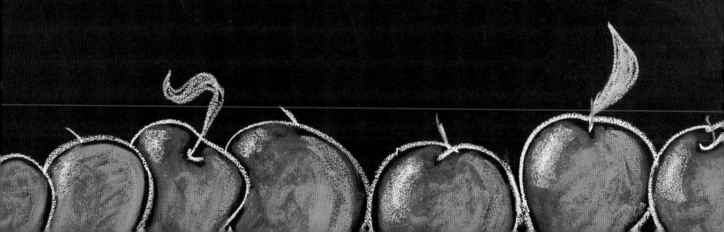

Summer Mango Salad

1 baby cos lettuce
1 mango, cut into 2cm dice
1 Lebanese cucumber,
  cut into batons
4oz (125g) mini Roma
  tomatoes, halved
½ avocado, diced
¼ cup mint leaves, torn
2 tablespoons slivered
  almonds, toasted
1 tablespoon extra virgin olive
  oil

1. Tear cos into bite-size pieces. Combine with mango, cucumber, tomatoes, avocado, mint and almonds. Drizzle with olive oil.

Serves 4

Cabbage Carrot and Seed Salad

1 carrot, grated

¼ small cabbage, finely
  shredded

1 tablespoon sesame seeds

½ tablespoon poppy seeds

¼ small bunch chives,
  chopped

DRESSING

1 tablespoon oil

½ tablespoon lemon juice

1 tablespoon natural yoghurt

¼ teaspoon mustard powder

1. Combine, carrot, cabbage, sesame seeds and poppy seeds in a bowl and mix well.
2. Place dressing ingredients in a small bowl and whisk well to combine. Pour over salad and stir through.
3. Sprinkle chives on top to serve.

Serves 4

Fattoush Salad

½ large, round piece
  Lebanese bread
1 butter lettuce, torn into
  bite-size pieces
4 radishes, trimmed
  and thinly sliced
1 Lebanese cucumber, peeled,
  deseeded and diced
8 cherry tomatoes, halved
1 teaspoon sumac
1 tablespoon olive oil
2 teaspoons lemon juice

1. Preheat oven to 350°F (180°C).
2. Tear the bread into bite-size pieces, place on a baking tray and toast in oven for 5 minutes or until golden.
3. Combine the lettuce, radishes, cucumber and tomatoes in a bowl. Add the toasted bread.
4. Combine the sumac, olive oil and lemon juice in a screw-top jar and shake well. Pour over dressing before packing into lunchbox, or send the dressing separately.

Serves 2

Couscous Salad with Currants

½ cup couscous

¹/₃oz (10g) butter, diced

¼ cup currants

¼ cup dried apricots, chopped

¼ cup mint, roughly chopped

¼ cup flat-leaf parsley, roughly chopped

1. Place the couscous in a heatproof bowl and pour over ½ cup of boiling water. Cover the bowl with cling wrap and set aside.

2. After 5 minutes, uncover the couscous and use a fork to break up the grains, then add the butter and stir through. Cool to room temperature. Add the remaining ingredients and gently stir. Refrigerate until ready to pack into lunchbox.

Serve 4

Smoked Chicken and Rice Salad

1 small smoked chicken
  breast, shredded
¾ cup jasmine rice, cooked
¼ cup sweetcorn kernels
¼ cup peas
½ green bell pepper
  (capsicum), finely diced
1 tomato, deseeded
  and finely diced
1 lime, quartered

1. Combine all ingredients except lime in a bowl and toss to combine. Serve with a wedge of lime in the lunchbox.

Serves 4

Smoked Salmon Bagel

2 bagels

2 tablespoons light cream cheese

¾oz (25g) rocket (arugula)

½ Lebanese cucumber

2 slices smoked salmon

1. Cut bagels in half and toast lightly. Spread the bottom halves with cream cheese, then top with rocket.

2. Using a vegetable peeler, peel strips of cucumber and place on top of rocket. Add the smoked salmon, top with remaining bagel halves and cut in half.

Makes 2

Winter Warmers

Winter is a time for hearty food and keeping warm. In this chapter, we provide you with lunches that can be eaten straight from the lunchbox, or warmed up in a pie warmer, microwave oven or sandwich press, if available. Perfect food for eating while wearing mittens and a scarf, and great for keeping out the chill.

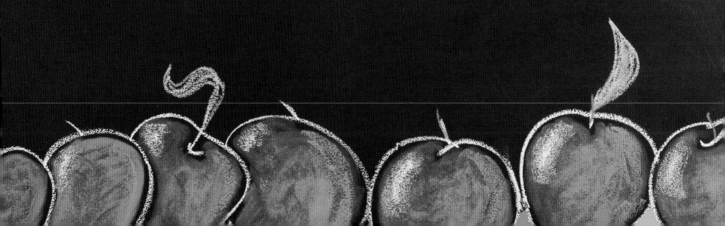

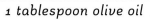

Pumpkin Soup with Star Puffs

1 tablespoon olive oil

1 small brown onion, chopped

1 leek, chopped

1 clove garlic, crushed

45oz (1.25kg) butternut
  pumpkin, peeled and cut into
  ¾in (2cm) pieces

4 cups vegetable stock

1 sheet ready-rolled puff
  pastry

¼ cup milk

1 tablespoon sesame seeds

salt and freshly ground
  black pepper

1. Preheat oven to 350°F (180°C).
2. Heat oil in a large saucepan over medium heat.
   Add onion, leek and garlic. Cook, stirring, for 5
   minutes, until leek becomes tender.
3. Add pumpkin and stock. Cover and cook for
   20–25 minutes or until pumpkin is tender.
4. Meanwhile, using a star shape cutter, cut stars
   from the pastry, brush with milk and sprinkle
   with sesame seeds. Place on an oven tray and
   cook for 10–15 minutes until golden and puffed.
5. When cooked, blend soup in batches. Return to
   saucepan and heat over medium heat until hot.
   Season to taste with salt and pepper.

Serves 4

Salami and Swiss Melt

1 piece Turkish bread

1 slice Swiss cheese, cut in half

¾oz (25g) baby spinach

4 slices mild salami

1 small tomato, thickly sliced

1 piece roasted capsicum

1. Preheat a sandwich press.
2. Cut the Turkish bread in half horizontally. Place one half of Swiss cheese on the bottom of the bread, top with spinach, salami, tomato, capsicum and remaining Swiss cheese. Cook in the sandwich press until cheese is melted and bread toasted.

Makes 1

Cheesy Ham Pasta Bakes

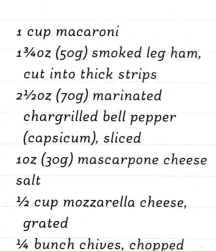

1 cup macaroni

1¾oz (50g) smoked leg ham,
   cut into thick strips

2½oz (70g) marinated
   chargrilled bell pepper
   (capsicum), sliced

1oz (30g) mascarpone cheese

salt

½ cup mozzarella cheese,
   grated

¼ bunch chives, chopped

1. Preheat oven to 400°F (200°C).
2. Bring a large saucepan of salted water to the boil, add the macaroni and cook for 8 minutes or until just firm in the centre (al dente). Drain, then return to the pan.
3. Add the ham, bell pepper and mascarpone and gently toss until just combined. Season with salt.
4. Spoon the pasta mixture into four ovenproof dishes and sprinkle with mozzarella. Bake for 10 minutes or until the cheese melts. Remove from oven and sprinkle with chives.

Serves 4

Homemade Baked Beans

1 tablespoon olive oil

1 brown onion, finely chopped

1 clove

14oz (400g) canned cannellini
   beans, rinsed and drained

14oz (400g) canned tomatoes,
   diced

1 tablespoon molasses

1 tablespoon brown sugar

1 bay leaf

salt and freshly ground
   black pepper

¼ cup parsley, chopped

1. Preheat oven to 350°F (180°C).
2. Heat oil in a large ovenproof casserole dish over medium heat. Add onion and cook, stirring, for 3 minutes or until tender. Add clove, beans, tomatoes, molasses, sugar and bay leaf. Season with salt and pepper. Stir well, then bring to the boil, reduce heat and simmer for 10 minutes.
3. Cover and bake for 30 minutes or until sauce is thick. Remove clove and stir through parsley.

Serves 4

Frittata

¹/₃oz (10g) butter

½ tablespoon olive oil

½ leek, white part only,
   thinly sliced

5oz (150g) button, Swiss brown
   or oyster mushrooms, sliced

3½oz (100g) baby spinach

4 eggs

¼ cup thickened cream

²/₃oz (20g) Parmesan cheese,
   grated

1 sprig basil, chopped

1. Preheat the oven to 350°F (180°C) and lightly butter a 5½in (14cm) square cake tin.
2. Melt butter with oil in a large frying pan over medium-low heat. Add leek and cook for 5 minutes until soft but not browned. Add mushrooms and spinach and cook for 5 minutes.
3. Meanwhile, whisk together eggs, cream and Parmesan. Place the leek mixture in the prepared tin, sprinkle with basil and pour over egg mixture. Bake for 25–30 minutes until lightly browned and set.
4. Cool slightly. Turn onto a board, and cut into squares.

Serves 4

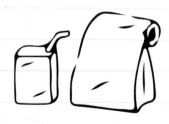

Chicken and Risoni Soup

1 small free-range chicken
   breast
1 tablespoon olive oil
1 small bulb fennel, finely
   chopped
½ carrot, peeled and
   finely chopped
½ courgette (zucchini), finely
   chopped
1 clove garlic, crushed
2 cups chicken stock
1¼oz (35g) risoni
1½oz (40g) peas
salt and freshly ground
   black pepper

1. Place chicken in a saucepan, cover with water and bring to the boil, turn heat down and lightly poach for 10 minutes until cooked. Drain and when cool enough to touch, shred.
2. Heat the oil in a saucepan over high heat. Add the fennel, carrot, courgette and garlic and cook, stirring, for 5 minutes or until just tender.
3. Add stock and bring to the boil. Add risoni and cook, stirring occasionally, for 8 minutes or until pasta is nearly al dente.
4. Add the peas and cook for 2 minutes or until bright green and tender. Remove from heat and stir through the chicken. Season with salt and pepper.

Serves 6

Pumpkin Pizza

2 small pizza bases
½ cup tomato pasta sauce
3½oz (100g) pumpkin, diced
  and roasted
1¾oz (50g) fetta cheese,
  crumbled
2 sprigs mint, chopped

1. Preheat oven to 350°F (180°C).
2. Spread pizza bases with the tomato sauce. Top
    with the roasted pumpkin, fetta and mint. Bake
    for 15–20 minutes until golden brown.

Serves 2

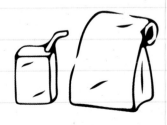

Lamb Kofta

9oz (250g) lean lamb mince
½ brown onion, finely diced
2 tablespoons couscous
2 sprigs mint, finely chopped
1 sprig parsley, finely
  chopped
2 teaspoon ground cumin
1 teaspoon ground coriander
1 tablespoon olive oil

1. Soak 10 skewers in water for 30 minutes.
2. Combine all ingredients in a mixing bowl. Mix together well, using hands.
3. Divide lamb mixture into heaped tablespoonfuls. Use wet hands to shape each portion into a sausage shape. Thread each kofta onto a skewer and place on a tray in a single layer. Cover and refrigerate for 1 hour or until firm.
4. Cook the koftas on a preheated barbecue grill or chargrill for 8–10 minutes or until just cooked through. Turn and brush with olive oil occasionally. Serve with pita bread and yoghurt.

Makes 10

Pig Pen

2 tablespoons vegetable oil

1 small onion, chopped

1 stalk celery, chopped

1 small leek, sliced

7oz (200g) canned chopped
   tomatoes

1 small carrot, chopped

1 small parsnip, chopped

1 small potato, diced

1¼ cups vegetable stock

salt and black pepper

2 Frankfurters, cut into small
   pieces (optional)

2 slices wholemeal bread

1. Heat 1 tablespoon of the oil in a heavy-based saucepan, then add the onion, celery and leek. Cook, covered, for 5 minutes or until softened, stirring occasionally.

2. Add the tomatoes, carrot, parsnip and potato, then cook for 3-4 minutes longer.

3. Pour the vegetable stock into the pan and season with black pepper and salt. Bring to the boil, cover, then simmer for 30 minutes or until the vegetables are tender. Remove from the heat and purée the soup with a hand blender until thick but still chunky, or mash with a potato masher. Add the Frankfurter pieces, if using, to the purée and heat through for 3 minutes.

4. Meanwhile, use a small pig-shaped pastry cutter to stamp out 6 'pigs' from the bread. Heat the remaining oil in a frying pan, then fry the bread pigs for 2-3 minutes on each side until golden. Drain on absorbent paper. Serve the pigs with the soup.

Serves 2

Pancake Stacks

²/₃ cup self-rising (self-raising) flour
2 tablespoons sugar
1 egg
²/₃ cup milk
1oz (30g) butter

1. Place flour in sifter or sieve. Sift into large mixing bowl. Add sugar.
2. Break egg into small bowl. Add milk. Whisk.
3. Make a well in centre of flour mixture. Pour in egg mixture. Beat with wooden spoon until smooth.
4. Place a little butter in frying pan. Heat over a medium-high heat until butter melts and sizzles.
5. Pour 3-4 tablespoons of batter into pan. Cook until bubbles form on top of pancake. Turn over. Cook for 1-2 minutes or until second side is brown.
6. Place cooked pancake on plate. Repeat with remaining pancake batter.
7. Stack three or four pancakes on each serving plate. Eat pancakes plain or top with your favourite topping.

Makes 10

Eggs in Ponchos

2 rashers back bacon,
  cut into small pieces
3 medium eggs
2 tablespoons milk
black pepper
1oz (30g) butter
¹/₃ cup canned chilli beans
2 wheat tortillas

GUACAMOLE
1 ripe avocado, chopped
1 small tomato, chopped,
  plus 1 tomato, cut into
  wedges
2 spring onions, finely
  chopped
juice of ½ lime
2 sprigs cilantro (coriander),
  chopped

1. To make the guacamole, place the avocado, chopped tomato, spring onions, lime juice and cilantro in a bowl. Mash with a fork to combine, then cover and set aside.

2. Place the bacon in a frying pan and fry in its own fat for 3 minutes or until crisp, then set aside. Mix the eggs and milk together with a fork, then season with pepper. Melt the butter in a non-stick saucepan. Add the egg mixture and cook, stirring, for 3 minutes or until the egg is scrambled and well cooked. Gently stir in the bacon pieces.

3. Meanwhile, heat the chilli beans in a saucepan for 4–5 minutes. Place a frying pan over a medium heat, then warm the tortillas, one at a time, for 15 seconds on each side. Transfer to plates, top with the scrambled egg and chilli beans, then wrap each tortilla loosely around its filling. Serve with the guacamole and tomato wedges.

Serves 2

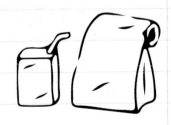

Hide and Seek

2 medium baking potatoes

1 tablespoon vegetable oil

2 rashers back bacon, cut into
  small pieces

2oz (60g) aged Cheddar
  cheese, grated

1 tablespoon crème fraîche

¼ small bunch fresh chives,
  chopped

salt and black pepper

COLESLAW

3½oz (100g) red cabbage,
  shredded

2 scallions (spring onions),
  chopped

1 apple, cored and chopped

1 small carrot, grated

2 tablespoons mayonnaise

1. Preheat the oven to 420°F (220°C). Rub the skins of the potatoes with oil. Bake the potatoes for 1 hour or until soft in the centre.

2. Place the bacon in a frying pan and cook in its own fat for 3 minutes or until crisp, then set aside.

3. To make the coleslaw, combine the cabbage, spring onions, apple, carrot and mayonnaise, and refrigerate until needed.

4. When the potatoes are cooked, slice the top off each one and reserve. Scoop out the centres and place in a bowl with the cheese, crème fraîche, chives and bacon pieces. Mix well with a fork and season with salt and black pepper. Pile the mixture back into the empty potato skins and return to the oven for 5 minutes to heat through. Replace the reserved potato tops over the filled potatoes and serve with the coleslaw.

Serves 2

Cheesy Potato Frittata

1 potato, cooked and cooled
2 rashers bacon
4 eggs
black pepper
1oz (30g) butter
²/₃oz (20g) aged Chedder
  cheese, grated

1. Cut potato into ¼in (1cm) cubes. Set aside.
2. Cut rind from bacon, then cut bacon into strips. Set aside.
3. Break eggs into bowl. Add black pepper to taste. Whisk, then set aside.
4. Place butter in frying pan. Heat over a medium heat until butter melts and sizzles. Add bacon and cook, stirring, for 2–3 minutes or until cooked.
5. Add potato to pan. Cook, stirring, for 5 minutes or until potato is brown.
6. Pour egg mixture into pan. Turn heat to low. Cook for 10 minutes or until frittata is almost set.
7. Preheat grill to high. Sprinkle top of frittata with cheese. Place pan under grill. Cook for 2–3 minutes or until cheese melts. Cut frittata into wedges to serve.

Serves 4

Pick-Up Sticks

¼ red bell pepper (capsicum),
   cut into small chunks
¼ yellow bell pepper
   (capsicum), cut into small
   chunks
4 button mushrooms,
   quartered
1 small courgette (zucchini),
   halved lengthwise and
   thickly sliced
3½oz (100g) tofu, cubed

MARINADE
1 tablespoon lemon juice
1 teaspoon liquid honey
2 tablespoons light soy sauce
black pepper

DIPPING SAUCE
1 teaspoon olive oil
1 small clove garlic, chopped
3 tablespoons plum sauce
1 teaspoon soft light brown
   sugar
¹⁄₃ cup vegetable stock

1. Soak 6 wooden skewers in water for 10 minutes to prevent them burning under the grill. To make the marinade, mix together the lemon juice, honey, soy sauce and black pepper in a large, non-metallic dish. Add the red and yellow bell peppers, mushrooms, courgette and tofu and stir to coat. Place in the refrigerator for 1 hour to marinate.

2. Preheat the grill to medium. Thread the vegetables and tofu onto the skewers. Grill for 6 minutes, turning skewers occasionally, until evenly cooked.

3. Meanwhile, make the dipping sauce. Heat the oil in a saucepan. Add the garlic and cook, stirring, for 1 minute or until softened. Stir in the plum sauce, sugar and stock and boil rapidly for 5 minutes or until the sauce has reduced and thickened slightly. Allow to cool for a few minutes, then serve with the kebabs.

Makes 6

Main Meals

Tasty Tacos

1 tablespoon vegetable oil

1 large onion, chopped

2 cloves garlic, crushed

17½oz (500g) lean beef mince

1oz (30g) packet taco
  seasoning mix

3 tablespoons tomato sauce

8 taco shells

4 large lettuce leaves, cut into
  strips

2 tomatoes, diced

1½oz (40g) aged Cheddar
  cheese, grated

1. Preheat oven to 350°F (180°C). Place oil in frying pan. Heat over a medium heat until hot. Add onion and garlic. Cook, stirring, for 5-6 minutes.
2. Add beef. Cook, stirring, for 5 minutes.
3. Stir in taco seasoning mix, ½ cup water and the tomato sauce. Cook, stirring for 5 minutes.
4. Place taco shells on baking tray. Heat in oven for 5 minutes.
5. Spoon beef mixture into taco shells. Top with lettuce, tomato and cheese.

Serves 4

Plough the Fields and Scatter

4oz (125g) potatoes, diced

1 tablespoon milk

1oz (30g) butter

2 teaspoons sunflower oil

1 onion, chopped

1 small clove garlic, crushed

1 carrot, diced

9oz (250g) minced lamb

8 sprigs mixed fresh herbs,
  such as thyme and rosemary

black pepper

½ cup lamb stock

dash of Worcestershire sauce

2 tablespoons fresh
  breadcrumbs

1oz (30g) aged Cheddar
  cheese, grated

1½oz (40g) frozen peas

¼ small bunch chives,
  chopped

1. Cook the potatoes in boiling water for 15 minutes or until tender, then drain. Mash with the milk and half the butter. Meanwhile, heat the oil in a heavy-based frying pan, add the onion and garlic and cook for 5 minutes or until softened. Add the carrot and cook for another 3 minutes to soften slightly.

2. Add the minced lamb and herbs to the onion and garlic and break up the mince with a wooden spoon. Cook for 10 minutes or until the mince has browned. Season, then add the stock and simmer, uncovered, for 20 minutes or until most of the liquid has evaporated. Add the Worcestershire sauce.

3. Preheat the grill to high. Mix together the lamb mixture and potatoes, then place in a flameproof dish. Sprinkle with the breadcrumbs and cheese. Drag the handle of a wooden spoon along the top to make furrows, then grill for 3-4 minutes, until golden. Meanwhile, fry the peas in the remaining butter for 1-2 minutes. Scatter over the 'field' with the chives.

Serves 2

Pot Plants

1 red bell pepper (capsicum)

1 yellow bell pepper
 (capsicum)

1 tablespoon balsamic vinegar

2 tablespoons olive oil

2 cobs baby corn

1 small onion, chopped

1 small clove garlic, chopped

2½oz (75g) minced lamb

1 teaspoon tomato purée

1oz (30g) bulgar wheat

½ cup lamb stock

1oz (30g) frozen peas

1oz (30g) dried apricots,
 chopped

1 teaspoon ground coriander

salt and black pepper

4 sprigs watercress

1. Preheat oven to 400°F (200°C). Slice off and discard the tops of the capsicums and deseed. Square off the bottoms and stand on a baking sheet. Sprinkle with the balsamic vinegar and 1 tablespoon of the oil. Cook for 15 minutes, then add the baby corn cobs to the sheet. Cook for 5–10 minutes, until everything is tender.

2. Meanwhile, heat the remaining oil in a large saucepan, add the onion and garlic and fry for 5 minutes or until softened. Add the minced lamb and cook for 5 minutes or until browned. Stir in the tomato purée, bulgar wheat, stock, peas, apricots and coriander, then season with salt and black pepper. Bring to the boil, then simmer for 15 minutes or until the stock has been absorbed, stirring occasionally.

3. Place the capsicum on plates and fill with the lamb mixture. Insert a baby corn and watercress sprigs into the top of each to serve.

Serves 2

Noodle Caboodle

4oz (125g) dried egg noodles
2 teaspoons vegetable oil
2 spring onions, chopped
1 small clove garlic, crushed
1 Lebanese cucumber, cut into
  thin sticks
2 cobs baby corn, sliced
4 cherry tomatoes
1¾oz (50g) smoked ham, cut
  into cubes
1 tablespoon light soy sauce
black pepper

1. Prepare the noodles according to the packet instructions, then drain well.
2. Heat the oil in a wok or large, heavy-based frying pan over a high heat. Add the spring onions, garlic, cucumber, corn, tomatoes and ham and stir-fry for 3 minutes or until the vegetables are tender and the tomatoes are beginning to split. Stir in the soy sauce and season.
3. Add the noodles to the vegetable mixture, toss well and stir-fry for 1-2 minutes, until heated through.

Serves 2

Jack and the Bean Pork

9oz (250g) potatoes, diced
1 small carrot, diced
½oz (15g) butter
black pepper
1 teaspoon vegetable oil
3 scallions (spring onions),
  chopped
1 small clove garlic, crushed
8 cocktail sausages or 4 pork
  sausages, halved crosswise
7oz (200g) canned ratatouille
4oz (125g) canned mixed
  beans, rinsed and drained
¾oz (25g) Cheddar cheese,
  grated
1 courgette (zucchini), cut into
  strips
8 snowpeas

1. Cook the potatoes and carrot in boiling water for 10–15 minutes until tender, then drain well and mash with the butter and pepper.
2. Heat the oil in a saucepan. Fry the scallions and garlic for 3 minutes or until softened. Add the sausages and cook for 10–15 minutes, until browned and cooked through. Stir in the ratatouille and beans and heat through, then season again.
3. Preheat the grill to medium. Transfer the sausage mixture to a flameproof dish, top with the mash and sprinkle with cheese. Grill for 3 minutes or until the cheese browns.
4. Meanwhile, cook the courgette strips and snowpeas in boiling water for 2 minutes to soften. Arrange the courgette strips on top of the pie in the shape of a beanstalk, using the snowpeas as leaves.

Serves 2

Honey Beef

1 tablespoon oil

17½oz (500g) lean rump steak,
   cut into thin strips

1 parsnip, cut into thin strips

1 red bell pepper (capsicum),
   cut into thin strips

4 spinach leaves, shredded

3 scallions (spring onions), cut
   diagonally into 1in (2.5cm)
   lengths

1 clove garlic, crushed

¾in (2cm) piece fresh ginger,
   grated

¹/₃ cup reduced-salt soy sauce

2 teaspoons cornflour blended
   with 2 tablespoons dry
   sherry

2 teaspoons honey

1. Heat half the oil in a frying pan or wok over a medium heat, add beef, parsnip, red capsicum, spinach and spring onions and stir-fry for 2–3 minutes or until meat changes colour. Remove mixture from pan and set aside.

2. Add remaining oil to pan and heat. Add garlic and ginger and stir-fry for 1–2 minutes, then return beef mixture to the pan. Combine soy sauce, cornflour mixture and honey, stir into pan and cook, stirring, for 1–2 minutes or until heated through. Serve immediately.

Serves 4

Chicken Satays

2 chicken breast fillets
3oz (90g) peanut butter
¼ cup coconut milk
1 tablespoon reduced-salt soy sauce
2 tablespoons vegetable oil

1. Cut chicken lengthwise into strips. Thread chicken onto bamboo skewers and cut off sharp ends.
2. Place peanut butter, ½ cup water, the coconut milk and soy sauce in a bowl and mix to combine. Brush mixture over chicken to coat.
3. Heat oil in a frying pan over a medium heat, add satays and cook for 2 minutes each side or until chicken is cooked and tender. Serve with rice.

Serves 4

Chicken Nuggets

17½oz (500g) ground (minced) chicken

1 egg, lightly beaten

1 cup breadcrumbs, made from fresh bread

2oz (60g) cottage cheese, mashed

¼ cup parsley, chopped

3 cups dried breadcrumbs

vegetable oil for shallow-frying

1. Place minced chicken, egg, fresh breadcrumbs, cottage cheese and parsley in a bowl and mix well to combine.

2. Take 2 tablespoons of mixture, shape into balls, then flatten slightly and gently press into dried breadcrumbs to coat. Repeat with remaining mixture.

3. Heat 1cm oil in a frying pan over a medium heat until hot, add nuggets and cook for 2 minutes each side or until cooked through and golden. Drain on absorbent paper, cool slightly and serve with tomato sauce.

Makes 24

Oven-Fried Chicken

½ cup natural yoghurt
1 teaspoon lemon juice
2 tablespoons apricot or
  peach chutney
3 cups dried breadcrumbs
6 chicken drumsticks
¼ cup parsley

1. Preheat oven to 350°F (180°C). Purée the yoghurt, lemon juice and chutney in a blender or food processor, then transfer to a shallow bowl. Spread out the breadcrumbs in a similar bowl.
2. Coat each drumstick in yoghurt mixture, then roll in breadcrumbs. Arrange on a baking sheet and bake for 45 minutes or until cooked through. Garnish with parsley and serve.

Makes 6

Crunchy Fish Sticks

3 potatoes, chopped
15oz (425g) canned tuna,
    drained and flaked
1 egg, lightly beaten
3 cups breadcrumbs, made
    from stale bread
vegetable oil for shallow-
    frying

1. Boil, steam or microwave potatoes until tender. Place in a bowl and mash until smooth. Add tuna and egg and mix well to combine.
2. Take 2 tablespoons of mixture, shape into thick fingers or sticks and press into breadcrumbs to coat. Repeat with remaining mixture.
3. Heat 1cm oil in a frying pan over a medium heat until hot, add fish sticks and cook for 3-4 minutes each side or until cooked through and golden. Drain on absorbent paper, cool slightly and serve.

Makes 24

Cheesy Salmon Patties

14oz (400g) canned butterbeans, drained

7oz (210g) canned red salmon, drained, bones and skin removed

4oz (125g) potato, boiled and mashed

3oz (90g) Cheddar cheese, grated

1oz (30g) Parmesan cheese, grated

1 small onion, finely chopped

¼ small bunch chives, chopped

1/3 cup all-purpose (plain) flour

2 tablespoons lemon juice

1 egg, lightly beaten

1½ cups dried breadcrumbs

oil for deep-frying

1. Mash butterbeans and salmon to a paste. Add potato, cheeses, onion, chives, flour and lemon juice. Mix well, then add enough egg to bind.
2. Divide mixture evenly into 6-8 portions and form each into a patty. Toss each patty in breadcrumbs until evenly covered.
3. Heat the oil in a large frying pan. Add the patties, pressing them down with a fish slice to flatten. Cook for 2 minutes on each side until golden.

Makes 6–8

Pansies

2oz (60g) sweet potato, diced

1 teaspoon sunflower oil, plus extra for brushing and deep-frying

2 scallions (spring onions), finely chopped

3½oz (100g) canned tuna, drained

1 tablespoon sweetcorn kernels

½ small red bell pepper (capsicum), finely chopped

dash of Worcestershire sauce

1 tablespoon all-purpose (plain) flour

1 tablespoon milk

black pepper

1 small beetroot or 1 large carrot, thinly sliced

1. Cook the sweet potato in boiling water for 10 minutes or until tender. Drain well, then mash. Heat the oil in a frying pan, add the spring onions and fry for 3 minutes or until softened.

2. Preheat the grill to medium. Place the sweet potato, spring onions, tuna, sweetcorn, red pepper, Worcestershire sauce and flour in a bowl and mix in the milk. Season with black pepper, then shape into 4 round cakes with your hands. Brush the tops with extra oil and grill for 5 minutes. Turn over, brush with oil again and grill for a further 5 minutes or until golden. Drain on absorbent paper and keep warm.

3. Meanwhile, heat 1in (2.5cm) of oil in a large saucepan. Fry the beetroot or carrot slices for 3–5 minutes, until crisp. Drain on absorbent paper. To serve, place 2 fish cakes on each plate and top each cake with 4–5 beetroot or carrot slices to make the pansy petals.

Serves 2

Little Fishes

½ cup long-grain rice

1 medium egg

7oz (200g) smoked haddock

¾ cup milk

¾oz (25g) cooked prawns,
 peeled

1 teaspoon lemon juice

pinch of nutmeg

pinch of curry powder

¼ cup parsley, chopped

3 tablespoons thickened
 cream

black pepper

½oz (15g) butter

2 slices bread

½ lemon, cut into quarters

1. Combine the rice with ¾ cup water in a
    saucepan. Bring to the boil, reduce heat to low,
    cover and cook for 15 minutes. Remove pan from
    heat, allow to stand covered for 10 minutes.

2. Meanwhile, hard-boil the egg for 10 minutes.
    Shell under cold water and finely chop. Put the
    haddock into a saucepan, cover with the milk
    and poach for 6-8 minutes, until just firm. Drain
    well, then flake the flesh, removing any bones
    and skin.

3. Preheat oven to 350°F (180°C). Place the egg,
    fish, rice and prawns in a bowl. Stir in the lemon
    juice, nutmeg, curry powder, parsley, cream and
    black pepper. Transfer to a buttered ovenproof
    dish. Dot the butter over the top, cover and cook
    for 25 minutes.

4. Meanwhile, toast the bread, then cut out fish
    shapes. Serve the rice dish with lemon wedges
    and the fish-shaped toasts.

Serves 2

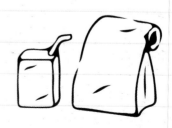

Starfish and Sea Chest

2 waxy potatoes, cut into
   1cm-thick chips

3½oz (100g) floury potatoes,
   diced

3½oz (100g) skinless cod
   fillets

½ cup milk

½ cup parsley, finely chopped

black pepper

1 small egg, beaten

2 tablespoons fresh
   breadcrumbs

3 tablespoons sunflower oil

4oz (125g) green cabbage,
   finely shredded

1. Place the waxy potatoes in a bowl of water. Boil the floury potato for 10 minutes or until tender, then drain and mash. Place the cod in a saucepan and cover with the milk. Poach for 5 minutes or until firm, then drain and flake, removing any bones.

2. Mix together the mashed potato, cod, parsley and black pepper. Divide the mixture in half and mould each half into a star shape, using your hands or a 3in (7.5cm) star-shaped cutter. Dip the starfish into the egg, then the breadcrumbs. Heat 1 tablespoon of the oil in a large, non-stick frying pan and cook the starfish for 5-7 minutes, turning once, until cooked and golden. Drain on absorbent paper and keep warm.

3. Heat the remaining oil in the frying pan until hot but not smoking. Drain the waxy potatoes, then dry the chips in a clean tea towel. Fry for 7–10 minutes, until cooked and golden, then drain on absorbent paper.

4. Meanwhile, steam the cabbage for 4-5 minutes until tender. To serve, build a square of chips to make a sea chest, then arrange the cabbage around the starfish like seaweed.

Serves 2

Speedy Salmon Rissoles

3 large potatoes, cooked and
  mashed
14oz (415g) canned pink
  salmon, drained and flaked
5oz (150g) pumpkin, grated
3 scallions (spring onions),
  chopped
1 tablespoon mild mustard
1 tablespoon natural yoghurt
1 egg white
2 teaspoons lemon juice
4oz (125g) wholemeal
  breadcrumbs, made from
  stale bread
2 teaspoons vegetable oil

1. Place potatoes, salmon, pumpkin, scallions,
   mustard, yoghurt, egg white and lemon juice in
   a bowl and mix to combine. Shape mixture into
   eight patties and roll in breadcrumbs to coat.
   Place patties on a plate lined with cling wrap
   and chill for 30 minutes.
2. Heat oil in a non-stick frying pan over a medium
   heat, add patties and cook for 3-4 minutes each
   side or until golden.

Serves 4

Satay Vegetables

2 teaspoons vegetable oil

12 snowpeas, trimmed and
  halved

15oz (425g) canned baby
  sweetcorn

2oz (60g) broccoli, chopped

½oz (15g) bean sprouts

¼ red bell pepper (capsicum),
  chopped

2oz (60g) peanut butter

1 tablespoon soy sauce

1. Heat oil in a frying pan over a medium heat, add
   snowpeas, sweetcorn, broccoli, bean sprouts and
   red pepper and stir-fry for 3 minutes.
2. Add peanut butter, soy sauce and ¼ cup water
   and cook, stirring, for 4 minutes longer or until
   vegetables are tender. Serve with noodles.

Serves 2–4

Two Foot Pie

½oz (15g) butter

1 small onion, finely chopped

1 small clove garlic, crushed

1 small parsnip, finely
chopped

1 small carrot, finely chopped

3½oz (100g) canned green
lentils, drained and rinsed

7oz (200g) canned chopped
tomatoes

1 tablespoon dried mixed
herbs

4 tablespoons vegetable stock

black pepper

1 small egg, beaten

'TWO FOOT' SCONES

3½oz (100g) self-raising flour

pinch of dry mustard

½oz (15g) butter, chilled and
cubed

1oz (30g) Cheddar cheese,
grated

4 tablespoons sour cream

1. Heat the butter in a frying pan, then add the onion and cook for 5 minutes or until softened. Add the garlic, parsnip and carrot and cook for a further 5 minutes until softened slightly. Add the lentils, tomatoes, herbs, vegetable stock and pepper to the pan and cook gently for 25 minutes, stirring occasionally, until the vegetables are tender.

2. Meanwhile, make the 'two foot' scones. Preheat the oven to 400°F (200°C). Sift the flour and mustard into a bowl. Rub the butter into the flour mixture with your fingertips until it resembles fine breadcrumbs. Add the Cheddar and sour cream, then mix with a fork to form a dough. Knead on a floured surface until pliable. Press or roll out to a thickness of ¼in (1cm), then shape into feet using your hands or a foot-shaped cutter.

3. Spoon the vegetable mixture into an ovenproof dish. Place the scone feet on top, then brush with beaten egg. Bake for 25 minutes or until the feet are well risen.

Serves 4

Veggie Bangers and Potatoes

1 large potato, cut into ¼in
  (1cm) slices
1 tablespoon vegetable oil
½ onion, chopped
4 vegetarian sausages,
  halved crosswise
1 small parsnip, sliced
1 apple, peeled, cored and
  sliced
1 small carrot, sliced
1 small courgette (zucchini),
  sliced
1 tablespoon tomato purée
¾ cup vegetable stock
½ cup apple juice
black pepper
1 tablespoon milk

1. Preheat oven to 375°F (190°C). Boil the potato slices for 10–15 minutes until just tender, then drain. Meanwhile, heat the oil in a heavy-based frying pan. Add the onion and sausages and fry for 5 minutes or until the onion has softened and the sausages have browned.

2. Add the parsnip, apple, carrot, courgette, tomato purée, vegetable stock and apple juice, then stir well. Season with black pepper, then transfer to an ovenproof dish. Arrange the potato slices over the top and brush with milk. Cook, covered, for 40 minutes. Raise the heat to 420°F (220°C), then uncover and cook for another 20 minutes to brown the potato.

Serves 2

Tomato Shells

2 tomatoes, halved

⅓ cup rice, cooked

¼ green bell pepper
  (capsicum), chopped

4 dried apricots, chopped

½ avocado, chopped

1 tablespoon mayonnaise

1. Cut off tops of tomatoes and scoop out flesh, leaving shells intact. Chop tops and flesh into pieces and place in a bowl.

2. Add rice, green bell pepper, apricots, avocado and mayonnaise and toss to combine. Spoon filling into shells.

Makes 2

Vegetables with Cheesy Potatoes

¼ cup olive oil

1 onion, chopped

1 aubergine (eggplant), cubed

1 green or red bell pepper
  (capsicum), chopped

2 courgette (zucchini), halved
  lengthwise and sliced

14oz (400g) canned chopped
  tomatoes, undrained

3oz (90g) green beans, halved
  or sliced

3oz (90g) butter or yellow wax
  beans, halved or sliced

¾ cup vegetable stock

1 tablespoon tomato paste

CHEESY POTATO TOPPING

17½oz (500g) potatoes,
  chopped

3-4 tablespoons milk

2oz (60g) aged Cheddar
  cheese, grated

1. Heat oil in a large saucepan over a medium heat, add onion and cook, stirring, for 3-4 minutes or until onion is soft. Add aubergine, cover and cook for 5 minutes.

2. Add green or red bell pepper, courgette and tomatoes to pan and cook, stirring occasionally, for 5 minutes. Add green beans, butter or yellow wax beans, stock and tomato paste and bring to a simmer. Simmer uncovered for 15 minutes or until vegetables are tender and mixture reduces and thickens.

3. To make topping, boil, steam or microwave potatoes until tender. Place in a bowl with milk and mash.

4. Transfer vegetable mixture to an oiled baking or casserole dish. Top with potatoes, sprinkle with cheese and bake for 15 minutes or until topping is golden.

Serves 4

Egg Foo Yung with Peas

2oz (60g) snowpeas, trimmed

2oz (60g) sugar snap peas, trimmed

3 eggs

½ teaspoon soy sauce

1 teaspoon sesame oil

1 tablespoon vegetable oil

1oz (30g) bean sprouts

1 scallion (spring onion), finely chopped

1. Boil, steam or microwave snowpeas and sugar snap peas until just tender. Drain, then refresh under cold running water, drain again and pat dry with absorbent paper.

2. Place eggs, ¼ cup water, the soy sauce and sesame oil in a bowl and whisk lightly to combine. Heat vegetable oil in a frying pan over a medium heat, add egg mixture and stir-fry for 1 minute, or until egg just begins to set. Add snowpeas, sugar snap peas, bean sprouts and scallion and stir-fry for 1 minute longer. Cool slightly and serve.

Serves 2

Vegetable Risotto

1 cup tomato or vegetable
  juice
½ cup vegetable or chicken
  stock
1 tablespoon vegetable oil
1 small onion, chopped
4oz (125g) carrots, finely diced
  or grated
2oz (60g) button mushrooms,
  sliced
1 cup Arborio rice
3oz (90g) courgette (zucchini),
  sliced
¼ red or green bell pepper
  (capsicum), sliced
1½oz (45g) aged Cheddar
  cheese, grated
toasted pinenuts or sesame
  seeds

1. Combine juice and stock in a saucepan and bring to a simmer.
2. Heat oil in a saucepan over a medium heat, add onion, carrots and mushrooms and cook, stirring, for 3-4 minutes or until onion is soft. Add rice, courgette and red or green bell pepper to the saucepan and cook over a medium heat, stirring constantly, for 3 minutes or until rice becomes translucent.
3. Pour ½ cup hot stock into rice mixture and cook, stirring constantly, until liquid is absorbed. Continue cooking in this way until all the stock is used and the rice is tender. Sprinkle with cheese and pinenuts or sesame seeds and serve.

Serves 4

Creamy Vegetable Pasta

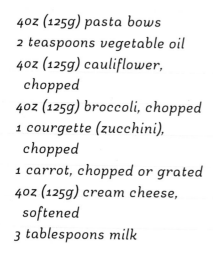

4oz (125g) pasta bows
2 teaspoons vegetable oil
4oz (125g) cauliflower, chopped
4oz (125g) broccoli, chopped
1 courgette (zucchini), chopped
1 carrot, chopped or grated
4oz (125g) cream cheese, softened
3 tablespoons milk

1. Bring a large saucepan of salted water to the boil, add the pasta and cook for 8 minutes or until just firm in the centre (al dente). Drain, set aside and keep warm.

2. Heat oil in a frying pan over a medium heat, add cauliflower, broccoli, courgette and carrot and cook, stirring, for 3-4 minutes or until vegetables are just tender.

3. Stir cream cheese and milk into pan and, stirring, bring to simmering. Simmer for 4 minutes. Spoon vegetable mixture over pasta and serve.

Serves 2

Mushroom Penne

4oz (125g) penne
1 tablespoon olive oil
4oz (125g) button mushrooms,
   sliced
2 tablespoons vegetable stock
2 tablespoons sour cream
8 sprigs fresh parsley,
   chopped

1. Bring a large saucepan of salted water to the boil, add the penne and cook for 8 minutes or until just firm in the centre (al dente). Drain, set aside and keep warm.

2. Heat oil in a frying pan over a medium heat, add mushrooms and cook, stirring, for 4 minutes. Add stock and sour cream to pan and cook for 2 minutes longer. Stir in parsley and spoon sauce over pasta. Toss to combine and serve.

Serves 1

Sweet Treats

Strawberry and Ricotta Muffins

2½ cups self-raising flour

1 teaspoon ground cinnamon

²/₃ cup superfine (caster) sugar

2 eggs

2oz (60g) unsalted butter, melted

1 cup milk

9oz (250g) ricotta cheese

9oz (250g) strawberries, quartered

1. Preheat oven to 350°F (180°C) and line a 12-cup muffin tray with cupcake cases.
2. Sift the flour and cinnamon into a large bowl. Add the sugar and stir to combine.
3. Place the eggs, butter and milk in a bowl and whisk to combine. Add to the dry ingredients and stir until just combined. Stir the ricotta and strawberries into the mixture, then divide between the muffin cups.
4. Bake for 20–25 minutes or until golden.

Serves 12

Rocky Road Ice Cream

36fl oz (1 litre) chocolate ice
cream, softened
2 x 2oz (60g) chocolate-
coated Turkish delight bars,
chopped
20 marshmallows, chopped
12 glacé cherries, chopped
2 x 1½oz (45g) chocolate nut
bars, chopped
1oz (30g) desiccated coconut

1. Place ice cream in bowl. Add Turkish delight
   bars, marshmallows, cherries, nut bars and
   coconut. Mix.
2. Spoon into an airtight container. Cover and
   freeze.

Serves 6

Muddy Puddles

2½oz (75g) chocolate digestive
  biscuits
2½oz (75g) butter
2½oz (75g) plain milk
  chocolate
2 tablespoons golden syrup
1 medium egg, beaten
few drops of vanilla extract
½oz (15g) white chocolate

1. Put the biscuits into a plastic bag, seal, then crush with a rolling pin. Melt 1oz (30g) of the butter in a saucepan. Remove from the heat and mix in the biscuits. Line a muffin tray with 4 paper muffin cases. Divide the biscuit mixture between them, pressing over the base and sides of each case with the back of a teaspoon. Refrigerate for 20 minutes or until firm.

2. Preheat the oven to 350°F (180°C). Put the remaining butter, milk chocolate and golden syrup in a bowl set over a saucepan of simmering water. Heat gently, stirring, until melted. Remove from the heat and cool for 5 minutes. Whisk in the egg and vanilla.

3. Spoon the chocolate mixture over the biscuit bases and bake for 20 minutes or until just firm. Leave to cool for 10 minutes. Meanwhile, melt the white chocolate in a bowl set over a pan of simmering water, then drizzle over the puddles.

Makes 4

Chocolate Brownie

7oz (200g) unsalted butter, chopped

7oz (200g) dark chocolate, broken into pieces

1 cup brown sugar

¾ cup gluten-free plain (all-purpose) flour

2 tablespoons cocoa powder

¾ cup walnuts, chopped

3 eggs, lightly beaten

1 teaspoon vanilla extract

¼ cup confectioners' (icing) sugar

1. Preheat oven to 375°F (190°C) and line a deep, 7in (18cm) square cake tin with baking paper.

2. Heat butter, chocolate and sugar in a saucepan over low heat, stirring constantly, until melted and smooth. Transfer to a bowl and set aside to cool slightly.

3. Sift flour and cocoa into a bowl, stir through walnuts. Add eggs and vanilla to chocolate mixture and mix well. Fold the dry ingredients through the chocolate mixture.

4. Pour brownie batter into the cake tin. Bake for 40-45 minutes or until just set, then allow to cool. Once cooled, lift out of tin and wrap in cling wrap. Place in an airtight container. Stand for 1 day before dusting with the icing sugar and cutting into pieces.

Makes 12 pieces

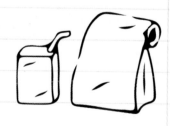

Banana and Date Bread

2 cups self-rising (self-raising) flour

1 teaspoon baking soda

pinch of salt

1 teaspoon ground cinnamon

½ cup superfine (caster) sugar

¾ cup fresh dates, chopped

2 eggs, lightly beaten

1 cup milk

2 ripe bananas, mashed

1. Preheat oven to 350°F (180°C), and line the base and sides of a 9 x 5in (23 x 13cm) loaf tin with baking paper.

2. Sift flour, baking soda, salt and cinnamon into a large bowl. Stir in sugar and dates.

3. Combine eggs, milk and bananas in a bowl and whisk until well combined. Stir egg mixture into dry ingredients until well combined.

4. Pour mixture into prepared loaf tin. Bake for 40-45 minutes, test with a skewer to make sure bread is cooked.

5. Leave to cool for 10 minutes, then turn onto a cooling rack.

Makes 1 loaf

INDEX

Published in 2012 by
New Holland Publishers Pty Ltd
London • Sydney • Cape Town • Auckland

Garfield House 86–88 Edgware Road London W2 2EA United Kingdom
1/66 Gibbes Street Chatswood NSW 2067 Australia
218 Lake Road Northcote Auckland New Zealand
Wembley Square First Floor Solan Road Gardens Cape Town 8001 South Africa

www.newhollandpublishers.com

A record of this book is held at the National Library of Australia and the British Library.

ISBN 9781742573649

Publisher: Fiona Schultz
Publishing director: Lliane Clarke
Designer: Stephanie Foti
Photography: R&R Publications
Production director: Olga Dementiev
Printer: Toppan Leefung Printing Ltd (China)

10 9 8 7 6 5 4 3 2 1

Keep up with New Holland Publishers on Facebook and Twitter.
www.facebook.com/NewHollandPublishers

UK £12.99
US $14.99